www.castlepointbooks.com

The Castle Point Books trademark is owned by Castle Point Publishing, LLC.
Castle Point books are published and distributed by St. Martin's Press.

978-1-250-27793-0 (paper over board)
978-1-250-27794-7 (ebook)

Design by Tara Long

Images used under license from Shutterstock.com

Our books may be purchased in bulk for promotional, educational, or business use.
Please contact your local bookseller or the Macmillan Corporate and Premium Sales Department
at 1-800-221-7945, extension 5442, or by email at MacmillanSpecialMarkets@macmillan.com.

First Edition: 2021

10 9 8 7 6 5 4 3 2 1

A very special thank-you to:

CONTENTS

LESSONS THAT LAST A LIFETIME

FROM THE DAY WE STEP INTO THEIR CLASSROOMS, teachers are there to help us reach our full potential. When we doubt ourselves, they assure us of our strengths. When we struggle to understand, they build a bridge to lead us across. And though we may be one of many students under their care, teachers always have a way of reaching out and making us feel like we truly matter.

Thank You for Teaching is a heartfelt tribute to the beloved educators who brighten the lives of their students and leave an impression that lasts a lifetime. More than a job, teaching is a calling. This collection of moving quotes celebrates the optimism and persistence of teachers, aids, tutors, professors, and educators who strive to make the world a better place, one student at a time.

Teachers have three loves:

LOVE OF LEARNING, LOVE OF LEARNERS, AND THE LOVE OF BRINGING THE FIRST TWO LOVES TOGETHER.

SCOTT HAYDEN

GOOD TEACHING IS MORE A GIVING OF *right questions* THAN A GIVING OF *right answers.*

JOSEF ALBERS

WHEN ONE TEACHES, *two learn.*

ROBERT HEINLEIN

TEACHING IS THE HIGHEST FORM OF
understanding.

ARISTOTLE

THE TEACHER WHO IS INDEED WISE *does not bid you* TO ENTER THE HOUSE OF HIS WISDOM *but rather leads you* TO THE THRESHOLD OF YOUR MIND.

KHALIL GIBRAN

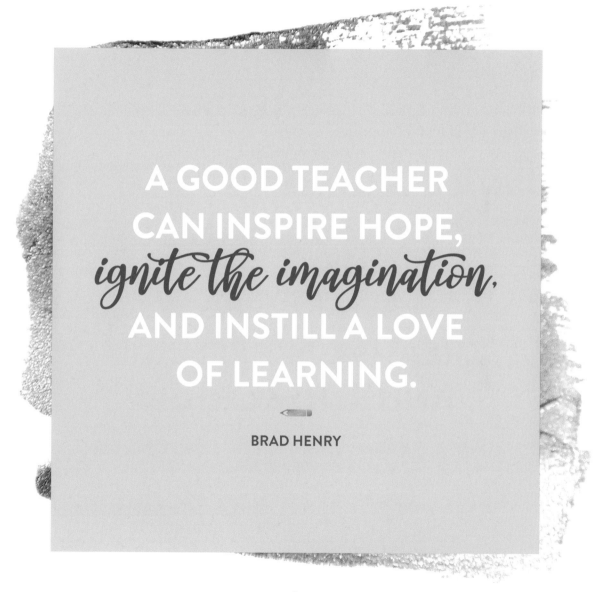

A GOOD TEACHER
CAN INSPIRE HOPE,
ignite the imagination,
AND INSTILL A LOVE
OF LEARNING.

BRAD HENRY

IT IS THE
supreme art
OF THE TEACHER
TO AWAKEN JOY IN
CREATIVE EXPRESSION
AND KNOWLEDGE.

ALBERT EINSTEIN

BEING ABLE TO HELP SOMEONE

learn something

IS A TALENT.

MARGARET RIEL

WHAT WE LEARN
WITH PLEASURE

we never forget.

ALFRED MERCIER

THE IMPORTANT THING
IS NOT SO MUCH
THAT EVERY CHILD
should be taught,
AS THAT EVERY CHILD
SHOULD BE GIVEN
the wish to learn.

JON LUBBOCK

NINE-TENTHS
OF EDUCATION IS
encouragement.

ANATOLE FRANCE

BETTER THAN A THOUSAND DAYS OF DILIGENT STUDY IS ONE DAY WITH *a great teacher.*

JAPANESE PROVERB

TEACHING IS
the greatest act
OF OPTIMISM.

COLLEEN WILCOX

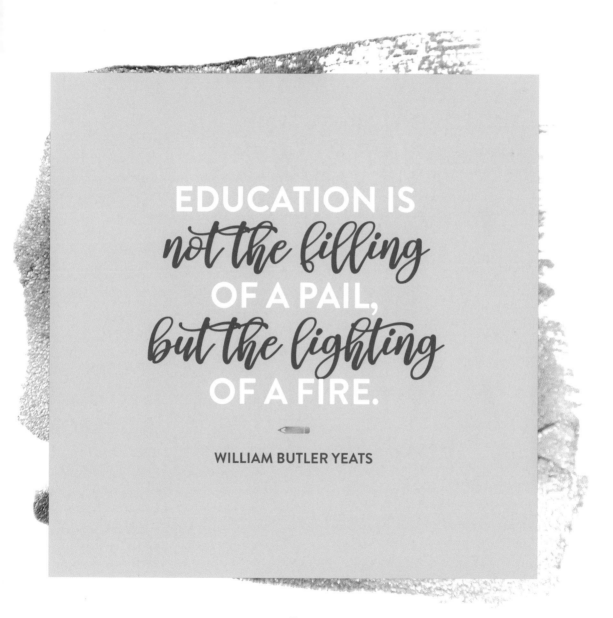

EDUCATION IS *not the filling* **OF A PAIL,** *but the lighting* **OF A FIRE.**

WILLIAM BUTLER YEATS

A great teacher IS SOMEONE WHO CAN LEARN FROM HIS STUDENTS, WHO CAN LEARN WITH THEM, AND LEARNS FOR THEM.

ROBERT JOHN MEEHAN

Unsettle
THEIR MINDS,
widen
THEIR HORIZONS,
inflame
THEIR INTELLECTS.

ROBERT M. HUTCHINS

SEEING THE BEST IN EVERYONE

GREAT TEACHERS EMPATHIZE WITH KIDS, RESPECT THEM, AND BELIEVE THAT *each one has something special* THAT CAN BE BUILT UPON.

✏️

ANN LIEBERMAN

THE JOB OF AN EDUCATOR IS TO TEACH STUDENTS *to see vitality* IN THEMSELVES.

JOSEPH CAMPBELL

I'VE LEARNED THAT
PEOPLE WILL FORGET
what you said,
PEOPLE WILL FORGET
what you did,
BUT PEOPLE WILL
NEVER FORGET HOW
you made them feel.

MAYA ANGELOU

THE GREAT TEACHER IS NOT THE MAN WHO SUPPLIES THE MOST FACTS, BUT THE ONE IN WHOSE PRESENCE *we become different people.*

RALPH WALDO EMERSON

A TEACHER
MUST BELIEVE IN THE
value and interest
of his subject
AS A DOCTOR
BELIEVES IN HEALTH.

GILBERT HIGHET

A GREAT TEACHER
takes a hand,
OPENS A MIND, AND
touches a heart.

UNKNOWN

TEACHERS
can change lives
WITH JUST THE
RIGHT MIX
OF CHALK AND
CHALLENGES.

JOYCE MEYER

The older I got,
THE SMARTER
MY TEACHERS
BECAME.

ALLY CARTER

TO THE WORLD
YOU MAY BE
JUST A TEACHER BUT
TO YOUR STUDENTS

you are a hero.

UNKNOWN

THE DUTIES OF A TEACHER ARE NEITHER FEW NOR SMALL, BUT THEY *elevate the mind* AND GIVE ENERGY TO THE CHARACTER.

DOROTHEA DIX

TEACHING KIDS TO COUNT IS FINE, BUT TEACHING THEM *what counts* IS BEST.

BOB TALBERT

A TEACHER'S JOB IS TO TAKE A BUNCH OF LIVE WIRES AND SEE THAT THEY ARE *well-grounded.*

DARWIN MARTIN

THE BEST TEACHERS ARE THOSE WHO SHOW YOU *where to look,* BUT DON'T TELL YOU *what to see.*

ALEXANDRA K. TRENFOR

TEACHING MIGHT EVEN BE THE *greatest of the arts* SINCE THE MEDIUM IS THE HUMAN MIND AND SPIRIT.

JOHN STEINBECK

WHAT SCULPTURE IS TO A BLOCK OF MARBLE, *education is to a soul.*

JOSEPH ADDISON

THE ART OF TEACHING IS THE ART OF
assisting discovery.

MARK VAN DOREN

I LIKE A TEACHER WHO GIVES YOU SOMETHING TO TAKE HOME TO THINK ABOUT

besides homework.

LILY TOMLIN AS EDITH ANN

GOOD TEACHERS KNOW HOW TO
bring out the best
IN STUDENTS.

CHARLES KURALT

BUILDING
BRIGHT
FUTURES

THE MEDIOCRE TEACHER TELLS.
THE GOOD TEACHER EXPLAINS.
THE SUPERIOR TEACHER DEMONSTRATES.
The great Teacher inspires.

WILLIAM ARTHUR WARD

A TRULY SPECIAL TEACHER IS VERY WISE, AND SEES TOMORROW *in every child's eyes.*

UNKNOWN

ONCE SHE KNOWS
HOW TO READ
THERE'S ONLY ONE THING
YOU CAN TEACH HER
TO BELIEVE IN AND
that is herself.

VIRGINIA WOOLF

MOST OF US
END UP WITH NO MORE
THAN FIVE OR SIX PEOPLE
WHO REMEMBER US.
TEACHERS HAVE

thousands of people
who remember them

FOR THE REST
OF THEIR LIVES.

A GIFTED TEACHER IS NOT ONLY PREPARED TO MEET THE NEEDS OF TODAY'S CHILD, BUT IS ALSO PREPARED *to foresee the hopes and dreams* IN EVERY CHILD'S FUTURE.

ROBERT JOHN MEEHAN

THE DREAM BEGINS WITH A TEACHER WHO BELIEVES IN YOU, WHO TUGS AND PUSHES AND LEADS YOU TO THE NEXT PLATEAU, SOMETIMES POKING YOU WITH A SHARP STICK *called truth.*

DAN RATHER

A TEACHER PLANTS THE
seeds of knowledge,
SPRINKLES THEM
WITH LOVE, AND
PATIENTLY NURTURES
THEIR GROWTH
TO PRODUCE
TOMORROW'S DREAMS.

UNKNOWN

The beautiful thing
ABOUT LEARNING
IS THAT NO ONE
CAN TAKE IT
AWAY FROM YOU.

B. B. KING

TRUE TEACHERS
ARE THOSE WHO
use themselves as bridges
OVER WHICH THEY
INVITE THEIR STUDENTS
TO CROSS; THEN, HAVING
FACILITATED THEIR CROSSING,
JOYFULLY COLLAPSE,
ENCOURAGING THEM
TO CREATE THEIR OWN.

NIKOS KAZANTZAKIS

IF YOU WERE SUCCESSFUL,
SOMEBODY ALONG
THE LINE GAVE
YOU SOME HELP.
THERE WAS
a great teacher
SOMEWHERE IN
YOUR LIFE.

BARACK OBAMA

A GOOD TEACHER
IS LIKE A CANDLE—
IT CONSUMES ITSELF
to light the way for others.

MUSTAFA KEMAL ATATURK

BE A WONDERFUL ROLE MODEL BECAUSE

you will be the window

THROUGH WHICH MANY CHILDREN WILL SEE THEIR FUTURE.

THOMAS MCKINNON

THERE IS NO SYSTEM
IN THE WORLD OR ANY
SCHOOL IN THE COUNTRY
THAT IS BETTER THAN
ITS TEACHERS.
Teachers are the lifeblood.
OF THE SUCCESS
OF SCHOOLS.

KEN ROBINSON

OUR TASK ...
IS TO HELP CHILDREN
*climb their
own mountains,*
AS HIGH AS POSSIBLE.
NO ONE CAN DO MORE.

LORIS MALAGUZZI

TO TEACH IS
TO TOUCH A LIFE
forever.

WHAT A TEACHER WRITES ON THE BLACKBOARD OF LIFE CAN

never be erased.

UNKNOWN

CREATING A BETTER WORLD

I AM NOT A TEACHER, BUT AN

awakener.

ROBERT FROST

THE TASK OF THE MODERN EDUCATOR IS NOT TO CUT DOWN JUNGLES BUT TO *irrigate deserts.*

C. S. LEWIS

ONE CHILD, ONE TEACHER, ONE BOOK, ONE PEN CAN *change the world.*

MALALA YOUSAFZAI

FREE THE CHILD'S POTENTIAL, AND YOU WILL *transform him* INTO THE WORLD.

MARIA MONTESSORI

A TEACHER

affects eternity;

HE CAN NEVER TELL WHERE HIS INFLUENCE STOPS.

HENRY ADAMS

EDUCATION IS FOR IMPROVING THE LIVES OF OTHERS AND FOR LEAVING YOUR COMMUNITY AND WORLD *better than you found it.*

MARIAN WRIGHT EDELMAN

NOT ALL SUPERHEROES WEAR CAPES, SOME HAVE *teaching degrees.*

UNKNOWN

TEACHERS ARE OUR
greatest public servants;
THEY SPEND THEIR LIVES EDUCATING OUR YOUNG PEOPLE AND SHAPING OUR NATION FOR TOMORROW.

SOLOMON ORTIZ

IT IS GREATER WORK
to educate a child,
IN THE TRUE AND LARGER SENSE OF THE WORLD, THAN TO RULE A STATE.

WILLIAM ELLERY CHANNING

EDUCATION IS THE

most powerful weapon

WHICH YOU CAN USE
TO CHANGE THE WORLD.

NELSON MANDELA

THE TEACHING PROFESSION CONTRIBUTES MORE *to the future of our society* THAN ANY OTHER SINGLE PROFESSION.

JOHN WOODEN

TEACHERS ...
ARE THE MOST
responsible and important
members of society
BECAUSE THEIR
PROFESSIONAL EFFORTS
AFFECT THE FATE
OF THE EARTH.

HELEN CALDICOTT, M.D.

EDUCATION BREEDS CONFIDENCE. CONFIDENCE BREEDS HOPE.

Hope breeds peace.

CONFUCIUS

IF YOU ARE PLANNING
FOR A YEAR, SOW RICE;
IF YOU ARE PLANNING FOR
A DECADE, PLANT TREES;
IF YOU ARE PLANNING
FOR A LIFETIME,
educate people.

CHINESE PROVERB

BE DILIGENT IN BELIEVING THAT WHAT WE DO IN THE CLASSROOM COULD POSSIBLY ECHO FOR A LIFETIME IN *the heart of a student.*

ROBERT JOHN MEEHAN

A GOOD EDUCATION
CAN CHANGE ANYONE,
a good teacher
CAN CHANGE
EVERYTHING.

UNKNOWN

THE HEART OF A TEACHER

YOUR HEART IS SLIGHTLY BIGGER THAN THE AVERAGE HUMAN HEART, BUT THAT'S BECAUSE *you're a teacher.*

AARON BACALL

TEACHING IS
NOT JUST A JOB.
It is a human service,
AND IT MUST BE
THOUGHT OF
AS A MISSION.

RALPH TYLER

EVERYONE WHO
REMEMBERS HIS
OWN EDUCATION
remembers teachers,
NOT METHODS
AND TECHNIQUES.
THE TEACHER IS
THE HEART OF THE
EDUCATIONAL SYSTEM.

SIDNEY HOOK

TECHNOLOGY IS JUST A TOOL. IN TERMS OF GETTING THE KIDS WORKING TOGETHER AND MOTIVATING THEM, *the teacher is* THE MOST IMPORTANT.

BILL GATES

ANYONE WHO DOES ANYTHING TO HELP A CHILD IN HIS LIFE

is a hero to me.

FRED ROGERS

THE BEST
TEACHERS
teach from the heart,
NOT FROM
THE BOOK.

UNKNOWN

ONE LOOKS BACK
WITH APPRECIATION TO
THE BRILLIANT TEACHERS,
but with gratitude
TO THOSE WHO TOUCHED
OUR HUMAN FEELINGS.

CARL JUNG

IN A COMPLETELY RATIONAL SOCIETY, *the best of us would be teachers* AND THE REST OF US WOULD HAVE TO SETTLE FOR SOMETHING ELSE.

LEE IACOCCA

**STUDENTS DON'T CARE
HOW MUCH YOU KNOW
UNTIL THEY KNOW**
how much you care.

JOHN C. MAXWELL

TEACHERS TEACH
because they care.
TEACHING YOUNG PEOPLE
IS WHAT THEY DO BEST.
IT REQUIRES
LONG HOURS,
PATIENCE, AND CARE.

HORACE MANN

A teacher is a compass
THAT ACTIVATES THE
MAGNETS OF CURIOSITY,
KNOWLEDGE,
AND WISDOM
IN THE PUPILS.

EVER GARRISON

What a teacher is,
IS MORE IMPORTANT
THAN WHAT
HE TEACHES.

KARL MENNINGER

IT TAKES A
big heart
TO HELP SHAPE
LITTLE MINDS.

UNKNOWN